MASONS

by Dr. Harold J. Berry

Former Professor of Bible & Greek
Grace University
Omaha, Nebraska

BACK TO THE BIBLE® Publishing

MASONS
published by Back to the Bible
©1990, revised 1999 by Harold J. Berry.
All rights reserved.

International Standard Book Number
0-8474-0828-0

For information:
BACK TO THE BIBLE
POST OFFICE BOX 82808
LINCOLN, NEBRASKA 68501

Printed in the USA

MASONS

Masons seem to be everywhere. They appear at public functions, such as the dedications of buildings, and seem to be involved in all aspects of life, up to and including the funeral service for their "Brothers." Besides being involved in many other organizations, Masons are found in churches of most denominations. In churches with liberal theology, one would not expect concern over theological differences, but in the theologically conservative Southern Baptist Convention alone, "14 percent of SBC pastors and 18 percent of deacon board chairs are Masons."[1] It is estimated that there are about 3.5 million Masons in the United States.[2]

Although only men can be Masons, related organizations are available for their relatives. The Order of the Eastern Star can include both men and women. DeMolay is for young men, and Rainbow Girls and Job's Daughters are for young women.

Many other secret societies seem to be patterned after the Masons. L. James Rongstad says, "[Freemasonry] is the 'Granddaddy' of all lodges. Its teachings, rituals, customs, and practices, and its secrecy have had an inspirational effect on other similar groups such as the Moose, Eagles, Elks, and the National Grange."[3]

William J. Whalen, author of *Handbook of Secret Organizations*, refers to other groups influenced by the Masons—including college fraternities. Whalen quotes William H. Shideler, founder of Phi Kappa Tau and a Mason himself, who stated, "Most of the rituals of college fraternities are based more or less directly upon the . . . Masonic ritual."[4]

Some people even think that the symbols on the back of the U.S. dollar bill have their origin in—or at least relate to—Freemasonry. The pyramid, the all-seeing eye, the number of feathers on the eagle's spread wings, the stars above the eagle's head in the shape of the Star of David, and the mottoes *e pluribus unum* (out of many one) and *novus ordo seclorum* (a new order of the ages) are believed to have obvious connections to Freemasonry.[5] This is difficult to prove, however.

The Masons are involved in many worthy causes. The public is perhaps most aware of the Shriners because of their entertaining and colorful involvement in parades. The most distinctive symbol of the Shriner is his red fez hat with the black tassel. To be a Shriner, a person must be a 32nd Degree Scottish Rite Mason or its equivalent in the York Rite (Knights Templar).

Shriners Hospitals for Crippled Children in the United States, Canada and Mexico have been of enormous help to many families. These orthopedic and burn hospitals are free to those

18 and under who might not otherwise be able to obtain treatment. While I was attending Dallas Theological Seminary, my wife worked as a registered nurse in the Texas Scottish Rite Hospital for Crippled Children in Dallas. She was highly impressed with the quality of care and concern given to children by that orthopedic hospital.

According to their own testimony: "Masons practice charity and benevolence and strive to promote human welfare. All over the world Masons care for their indigent Brethren, widows and orphans; maintain homes; support their mother countries in great wars; aid medical research, gerontology, blood banks, youth programs, military rehabilitation; contribute scholarships and practice character building."[6]

"What," you ask, "can possibly be wrong with an organization that does all of that?" People differ on their answers to that question.

Some think Freemasonry is only a fraternal or social organization. As such, they see no problem with a Christian being a Mason. Others are greatly concerned about the beliefs of Freemasonry and maintain that its views are in open conflict with biblical Christianity.

Local churches can face difficult decisions when receiving new members or considering members for leadership positions. How significant is it to the church that a person is a Mason?

It is important to compare the teachings of Masonry with the Bible, the written revelation of God. For only then can the question be answered: Can a knowledgeable and committed Mason be a knowledgeable and committed Christian?

There is no intent to reveal in these pages any "secrets" of the Masonic Lodge. If such is done, it will be unintentional—and unnecessary. If the published literature of the Masons clearly shows that their teachings are contrary to the teaching of the Bible, it does not matter what the secrets are.

Some Masons trace the origin of their organization back to the beginning of time, but most modern Masons are more moderate in their claims. Although much of their teaching is tied to Solomon's temple, which was erected during Old Testament times, modern Masonry dates only to 1717. It was in that year that four lodges in Great Britain formed the first Grand Lodge of England, which became known as the Premier Grand Lodge of the world.

The terminology and symbolism of Masonry seem to come mostly from the actual craft of stonemasonry during the Middle Ages. Stonemasons gathered as a union to develop their craft and keep secrets from others. It is uncertain where the *free* is derived from in the word *Freemasonry*. Some think it was used because masons worked with free-stones, or stones that could be cut without splitting. "Such workmen were first called masons of free stone, then, free stone masons, and finally freemasons."[7]

The term *free* in Masonry is also taught to mean "free-born"; that is, never having been a slave.

Those actually working with stone were known as "operative" masons. Later, when non-stone workers joined the group, they were referred to as "speculative" masons. "Speculative Freemasonry is also called symbolic Freemasonry, since the working tools of operative Masonry are used as symbols to teach moral and philosophical lessons."[8] These non-operative Masons were also referred to as "Accepted."

Stonemasons had three classifications for workers practicing their craft: Apprentice, Fellow Craft and Master Mason. This is also the terminology used for the first three degrees in Freemasonry.

Masons of the first three degrees form the Blue Lodge of Masonry. Blue apparently is symbolic of the sky, and so the Blue Lodge relates to universal Masonry. A man is not considered a full-fledged Mason until he has reached the Third Degree—Master Mason. In a sense, he can never be a higher Mason than he is after having received this Third Degree, even if he goes on to other degrees.

Once a man has become a Master Mason, he need not go any further; and apparently most do not. But those who wish to pursue more of the mysteries of Masonry—to search for greater light—can become a part of the Scottish Rite or the York Rite. The Scottish Rite offers degrees 4 through 32 (the 33rd Degree is honorary). The York Rite has fewer titles, but they are equivalent to various degrees of the Scottish Rite. For example, as mentioned previously, The Order of the Knights Templar of the York Rite is equivalent to the 32nd Degree of the Scottish Rite.

Masons claim they never invite anyone to join their membership—that it is necessary for an interested person to ask to become a member. There is a thin line, however, between merely telling a person the advantages of being a Mason and implying that he should become one. But Masonry says, "All you have to do is ask"—even using the passage from the Bible: "Ask, and it will be given you; seek, and you will find; knock, and it will be opened to you" (Matt. 7:7). A person must "ask" to be a candidate; then "knock, and it will be opened to you" is a prompt for the candidate to knock and gain admission to the lodge room.

Many allegories and symbols are used in Masonry. It is common for Masonic writers to refer to an ancient definition of their ancient craft: "Freemasonry is a system of morality, veiled in allegory, and illustrated by symbols."

To construct an adequate allegory or symbol, a person must have precisely in mind what he is endeavoring to allegorize or symbolize. But the Masonic "authorities" do not agree about what their allegories and symbols refer to. Carl Claudy, author of many books on Freemasonry, explains, "A symbol may have many meanings, all of them right, so long as they are not self-contradictory."⁹ Symbols can be made to mean almost anything a person chooses to make them mean.

While it is interesting to know how the Masonic Lodge got started, our chief concern should be the beliefs of Freemasonry. Do those beliefs conflict with biblical Christianity?

BELIEFS

Masonry is not just a social fellowship—it has a system of beliefs about cardinal doctrines of Christianity, including the source of authority, God, Jesus Christ, sin, salvation and the future life. It is apparent that Freemasonry is actually a religion.

As Elliot Miller, specialist in New Age beliefs, pointed out, "The U.S. Supreme Court has ruled that a primary characteristic of a religion is that it adheres to and promotes 'underlying theories' concerning such 'ultimate' realities as man's nature and his place in the universe."[10] This is certainly true not only of the New Age Movement but also of Freemasonry.

Though many Masons are unaware that Freemasonry is a religion, consider what some of their leaders say. Joseph Fort Newton (1880-1950), an Episcopal minister and recognized authority in the Masonic world, said, "Masonry is not a religion but Religion—not a church but a worship, in which men of all religions may unite."[11] Newton seemed to detract somewhat from his former statement when he later said, "Masonry is not a religion, but it is religious."[12]

Newton also wrote: "Religion, then, is the bond that binds us, first, to God, Whose [sic] is 'the something universal' *which unites all things into one whole,* and gives to the universe meaning and beauty. Second, it is the tie by which we are united to our fellow men in the service of duty, the sanctity of love, and the *spirit of fraternal righteousness*"[13] (emphasis mine).

The teaching that everything is of one essence is known as monism, from the Greek word for "one." This is the view of Hinduism, which has influenced so many religious groups in North America—such as Christian Science, Unity School of Christianity, Rosicrucianism and the New Age Movement. Also, righteousness—contrary to Newton's comments—is not obtained by fraternal relationships but by a relationship with a personal God. (See Romans 3:22.)

Henry Wilson Coil, born in 1885, was the author of the encyclopedia that many lodges now accept as their authoritative source. When John Ankerberg, host of the nationally televised "John Ankerberg Show," polled the Grand Lodges (there is one Grand Lodge in each state), 44 percent of those who responded recommended *Coil's Masonic Encyclopedia* as their authoritative source.[14]

Coil rejects any statement that says Masonry is not a religion—only religious. "It would be as sensible to say that man had no intellect but was intellectual or that he had no honor but was honorable."[15] Coil further comments, "If Freemasonry were not religion, what would have to be done to make it such? Nothing would be necessary or at least nothing but to add more of the same. That brings us to the real crux of the matter; the difference between a lodge and a church is one of degree and not of kind."[16]

Coil adds, "Freemasonry has a religious service to commit the body of a deceased brother to the dust whence it came and to speed the liberated spirit back to the Great Source of Light. Many Freemasons make this flight with no other guarantee of a safe landing than their belief in the religion of Freemasonry. If that is a false hope, the Fraternity should abandon funeral services and devote its attention to activities where it is sure of its ground and its authority."[17] These comments clearly show that Freemasonry is considered by some of its significant leaders to be a religion.

Freemasonry considers Christianity to be only one religion among many others, such as Judaism, Islam and Buddhism. Freemasonry also considers itself to be above these, for it supposedly holds the tenets to which most all religions subscribe—the Fatherhood of God, the brotherhood of man and the immortality of the soul. But is this biblical Christianity?

The answer is found as we examine the beliefs of Freemasonry concerning the source of authority, God, Jesus Christ, sin, salvation and the future life.

SOURCE OF AUTHORITY

In Freemasonry the Bible is called the "Volume of the Sacred Law" (sometimes abbreviated V.S.L.). The V.S.L. is an indispensable part of what is called "the furniture" in a Masonic Lodge.

North Americans are more impressed than they should be about the Lodge's use of the Bible. If they joined the Lodge in some other parts of the world, the V.S.L. would be something other than the Bible.

No better authority can be cited to confirm this than Albert Pike (1809-1901), who was responsible for virtually rewriting the Scottish Rite degrees into their present form. Pike said, "The Bible is an indispensable part of the furniture of a Christian Lodge, only because it is the sacred book of the Christian religion. The Hebrew Pentateuch in a Hebrew Lodge, and the Koran in a Mohammedan one, belong on the Altar; and one of these, and the Square and Compass, properly understood, are the Great Lights by which a Mason must walk and work."[18] Notice that the "Great Lights" include the Mason's tools of the square and compass as well as the Bible. No claim is made for the sole authority of the Bible as the only Great Light.

Knowledgeable Masons know how the Bible is viewed by Freemasonry. Carl Claudy agrees with Pike when he tells the Entered Apprentice, or one who has achieved the first degree, that the Bible is always referred to as "The Great Light" in this country, but "the practice may be and often is different in other lands. What is vital and unchangeable, a Landmark of the Order is that a *Volume of the Sacred Law be open upon the Masonic altar whenever the lodge is open.* A lodge wholly Jewish may prefer to use only the Old Testament; in Turkey and Persia the Koran would be used as the V.S.L. of the Mohammedan; Brahmins would use the Vedas"[19] (emphasis his). Where many races and creeds exist, as in the Far East, Claudy explains that some lodges provide several holy books for the initiate to make his choice.[20] It appears that Masonry does not care what book a person considers sacred or uses in his search for the light. Masonry's only concern is that each person must swear by the most holy book he knows that he will keep the oaths of Freemasonry.

In their excellent book *The Deadly Deception*, Jim Shaw and Tom McKenney expose Freemasonry for what it really is. Shaw was a 33rd Degree Scottish Rite Mason before he saw the darkness of Freemasonry and turned to the light by trusting the Lord Jesus Christ as his Savior. "Masonry, contrary to popular belief," Shaw says, "is NOT based upon the Bible. Masonry is actually based on the Kabala (Cabala), a medieval book of magic and mysticism"[21] (emphasis his).

According to *Coil's Masonic Encyclopedia*, the Kabala "contains the mystic lore of the Jews. . . . It contains both Babylonian mythological and Zoroastrian theological concepts."[22] Coil claims no relationship of the Kabala to Freemasonry "except that the originators of the *Hauts Grades* on the Continent of Europe resorted to it in search of ritualistic lore and the consequences will be observed in some of the mystical and philosophical degrees."[23]

Newton acknowledged that the "Square, Rule, Plumb-line, the perfect Ashlar, the two Pillars, the Circle within the parallel lines, the Point within the Circle, the Compasses, the Winding Staircase, the numbers Three, Five, Seven, Nine, the double Triangle—these and other such symbols were used alike by Hebrew Kabbalists and Rosicrucian Mystics."[24] Newton, however, did not believe Freemasonry borrowed these symbols from others; he claimed the others borrowed them from Freemasonry.[25]

Pike, however, was more emphatic than Coil and Newton about the importance of the Kabala. In explaining the Hebrew letter Yod (written like the English apostrophe) enclosed in a triangle, a symbol used in Masonic lodges, Pike said, "Yod is, in the Kabalah, the symbol of Unity, of the Supreme Deity, the first letter of the Holy Name; and also a symbol of the Great Kabalistic Triads. To understand its mystic meanings, you must open the pages of . . .

kabalistic books, and ponder deeply on their meaning."[26]

In explaining another symbol, Pike told the Entered Apprentice, "That meaning is not for the Apprentice. The adept [the one in possession of the secrets] may find it in the Kabalah."[27] Pike left no doubt about his belief that the Kabalah was the ultimate source of Masonic beliefs. He said, "Masonry is a search after Light. That search leads us directly back, as you see, to the Kabalah."[28]

Masons who think the Bible is taken seriously by Freemasonry as a guide of faith and practice do not know what their own leaders have written. Furthermore, the Freemasons' failure to accept the Bible as the only source of authority is seen in what they believe about God.

GOD

In today's theologically confused world, it is important to determine what is meant when a person, organization or fraternity uses the word *God*. Some groups (such as Christian Science, Unity School of Christianity and the Rosicrucians) perceive God to be a principle rather than a person with intellect, emotions and will. Transcendental Meditation and the New Age Movement—true to their Hindu origin—believe God to be an impersonal being or essence of the universe. What do the Masons believe about God?

This answer is especially important since no one can become a Mason unless he believes in God. (In fact, the Lodge accepts all but atheists—the main exception being the Utah Grand Masonic Lodge, which refuses to accept Mormons at any lodge in the state.)[29] Claudy emphasizes, "The petitioner knows it before he signs his application. He must answer 'Do you believe in God?' before his petition can be accepted. He must declare his faith in a Supreme Being before he may be initiated."[30]

This may impress many people that Freemasonry is biblical, but consider Claudy's following comments: "But note that he is not required to say, then or ever, *what* God. He may name Him as he will, think of Him as he pleases; . . . Freemasonry cares not"[31] (emphasis his).

Rather than even using the word *God*, the Masons more commonly refer to their deity by another expression—Great Architect of the Universe—usually abbreviated G.A.O.T.U.[32]

In the Fellow Craft, or Second Degree, deity is further explained as "God, Great Architect of the Universe, Grand Artificer, Grand Master of the Grand Lodge Above, Jehovah, Allah, Buddha, Brahma, Vishnu, Shiva, or Great Geometer[;] a symbol of the conception shines in the East of every American Masonic lodge, as in the center of the canopy of every English lodge."[33]

Many people see the Masonic ring, with its emblem of a compass and a square with the letter "G" in the center, and presume that the "G" refers to God. Although that is one of its symbolic meanings, the "G" can also refer to geometry—the science of the stonemason. Claudy quotes Plato, who said, "God is always geometrizing." Then Claudy adds, "It is merely an accident of the English language that geometry and God begin with the same letter."[34]

The Masons are fond of speaking of the Fatherhood of God, as in the expression, "There is one God, the Father of all men." In the sense that God created mankind, it is true that He is the Father of us all. But the Bible clearly distinguishes between those who have come into a right relationship with the Father and those who have not. Those outside of that relationship are not considered the children of God. Instead, they are known as the children of the Devil. Jesus told some unbelievers, "You are of your father the devil, and the desires of your father you want to do" (John 8:44). The Lord Jesus

Christ never spoke of the Fatherhood of God in the sense in which the Masons use the expression. But notice what the Masons believe about the Lord Jesus Christ.

JESUS CHRIST

Those who claim no conflict exists between the beliefs of Freemasonry and Christianity need to look more carefully at what some of the Masonic leaders have written. Historical Christianity believes that Jesus Christ is a triune member of the one Godhead, and as such He is God. The Lord Jesus Christ became a man that He might die for the sins of the world. Had He not become man, He could not have died for our sins. Had He not been God, His death could not have provided salvation for all who trust Him as Savior. But what does Freemasonry say to all of this?

It is interesting—and significant—to note that Joseph Fort Newton's book *The Builders* has no entry in the index for "Jesus" or "Christ." *Coil's Masonic Encyclopedia* has no such separate entry either, although he groups many elements under "Religion." Neither does Holman's Masonic Edition of the Holy Bible include an entry of either "Jesus" or "Christ" in its "One Hundred and Sixty Questions and Answers," which was compiled from the works of Albert Mackey and other eminent Masonic authorities in 1935. The closest this index comes to a direct reference to Jesus Christ is what is said under the entry "Lost Word." Mansonry claims that the actual name for "God" has been lost. Under this entry is posed the question: "What is the true meaning of the Lost Word?" The answer given is: "The true meaning of the Lost Word is Divine Truth, symbolically speaking. This is what the old writers claim and has reference to the Ineffable name. St. John 1:1."[35]

John 1:1 says, "In the beginning was the Word, and the Word was with God, and the Word was God." Masonry seems to believe that the reference to *Word* in this verse has to do with the lost word of God's "ineffable" name. But verse 14 explains what the "Word" of verse 1 refers to: "And the Word became flesh and dwelt among us, and we beheld His glory, the glory as of the only begotten of the Father, full of grace and truth." The "Word" clearly refers to the Lord Jesus Christ. But, of course, the Masons cannot acknowledge this, or it would offend the Jews, Muslims and members of other non-Christian religions who are allowed to be part of Freemasonry.

The Gospel of John records the words of Jesus, "I am the way, the truth, and the life. No one comes to the Father except through Me" (14:6). No one who is knowledgeable of and committed to Masonry can agree with Jesus' words. Freemasonry does not believe that Jesus Christ is God nor that salvation is available only through Him.

Freemasonry is a search for light. The Masons acknowledge that "light is a symbol of knowledge. It is the ultimate desire of every Mason to be well informed on Masonry, and may every Mason strive constantly for light, and especially for light eternal."[36]

But the Lord Jesus Christ said, "I am the light of the world. He who follows Me shall not walk in darkness, but have the light of life" (John 8:12).

Many references in the four Gospels speak of light as referring to the Lord Jesus Christ. John 1:1-18 sufficiently shows that any use of language that shows the light to be something other than the Lord Jesus Christ is a use of language that allows man to make up any meaning he wants.

Referring to the Hindu teaching of reincarnation and the Hebrew concept of the afterlife—which he thinks are founded on the same teaching—George H. Steinmetz reveals how Masonic thinking conflicts with biblical teaching: "Neither philosophy has ever taught of the coming of an INDIVIDUAL who would be the 'Savior,' the 'Messiah' or 'Redeemer.' When properly understood these great philosophies teach that through many incarnations and the slow process of evolution the ENTIRE HUMAN RACE is rising toward perfection. The Messiah, then, will be the final achievement of that 'plan' of the Supreme Architect—NOT AN INDIVIDUAL, but—THE PERFECTION OF THE RACE!"[37] (emphasis his).

Steinmetz adds, "It is not our intention to review the endless arguments as to the divinity of either Krishna or Jesus. Regardless of whether or not they were mystically conceived, there is little room for argument that the stories told about them and their legendary background partake of the incidents and are of the essence of the legend of the 'Dying God,' and it has been determined that the origin of that legend is the journey of the sun through the zodiacal signs of the heavens."[38]

When comparing the various religions and legends, Steinmetz sees little that is distinctive about Christianity. "Thus we discover that most of the events, the allegories and symbolism of the various 'Messiahs,' seemingly have their origin in that most ancient of religious beliefs—Solar Worship."[39]

Does Steinmetz think Solar Worship is also the origin of the teachings of Freemasonry? For instance, the legend of Hiram Abiff (whom Masons regard as the chief architect of Solomon's temple) is a major part of Masonry. What is its source? "There is a similarity between the Hiramic legend and these other legends," Steinmetz acknowledges, "but our ignorance of the origin of the former does not permit the categorical statement that it is taken from them; it may have its own particular line of descent directly from the Solar Myths."[40]

Although Steinmetz admits that the Hiramic legend is derived from Solar Myths, it is significant that he wishes to claim more distinctiveness for the Hiramic legend than for the beliefs of other world religions.

Former 33rd Degree Mason Jim Shaw says of Hiram Abiff: "It is the consensus of opinion among Masonic authorities, philosophers and writers of doctrine that the legend of Hiram Abiff is merely the Masonic version of a much older legend, that of Isis and Osiris, basis of the Egyptian Mysteries."[41]

When the Bible is used in Freemasonry, the references to Jesus Christ are omitted, lest other religions be offended. For instance, when 1 Peter 2:5 is used in a Masonic lodge, it is quoted as: "Ye also, as lively stones, are built up a spiritual house, an holy priesthood, to offer up spiritual sacrifices, acceptable to God" (KJV). But Masons deliberately omit the last three words of the verse: "by Jesus Christ." This shows the true attitude of the Lodge toward Christianity.

Also, although prayer pervades all the rituals of Masonry, they are Christless prayers. A well-ordered lodge never allows prayer to be offered in the name of Jesus Christ.

The Entered Apprentice is told: "In his private devotions a man may petition God or Jehovah, Allah or Buddha, Mohammed or Jesus; he may call upon the God of Israel or the Great First Cause. In the Masonic Lodge he hears humble petition to the Great Architect of the Universe, finding his own deity under that name. A hundred paths may wind upward around a mountain; at the top they meet."[42]

Freemasonry does not adjust its beliefs to fit the Bible; the Bible is adjusted to fit the beliefs of Freemasonry.

SIN

One must search hard to find references to sin in the writings of the Masonic leaders. It is only mentioned in passing as they discuss other topics. Masons are like Christian Scientists, the New Age Movement and Unity School of Christianity in this regard: They deny the reality of sin as mentioned in the Bible. They think that any short-comings can be overcome by greater enlightenment. When the Masons refer to sin, their comments are far from the biblical teaching on the subject.

The Bible clearly talks about the reality of sin and the penalty it carries with it. Romans 3:23 says, "All have sinned and fall short of the glory of God." Romans 5:12 says, "Just as through one man sin entered the world, and death through sin, and thus death spread to all men, because all sinned." Romans 6:23 says, "For the wages of sin is death," and the Bible teaches that both physical and spiritual death result from sin.

In answer to the question, "What is the symbolism of a Master Mason, and how is it represented?" the notes in the Holman Masonic Edition of the Bible say in part: "By its legend and all its ritual, it is implied that we have been redeemed from the death of sin and the sepulchre of pollution."[43]

SALVATION AND FUTURE LIFE

If sin and its penalty do not exist, we have nothing to be saved from. But if that were the case, Jesus would not have left His position with the Father to take upon Himself human form so that He could redeem mankind, as recorded in Philippians 2. Of course, for Masons this isn't a conflict since they don't believe in Jesus Christ of the Bible anyway.

All are guilty of sin; but fortunately, 1 John 2:1-2 says, "If anyone sins, we have an Advocate with the Father, Jesus Christ the righteous. And He Himself is the propitiation [satisfaction] for our sins, and not for ours only but also for the whole world." Any person may receive eternal life and forgiveness of sin by receiving Jesus Christ as Savior (John 1:12; Rom. 6:23). But what do the Masons propose as the means of salvation?

"What then is this thing called 'SALVATION'?" asks Steinmetz in *The Lost Word*.[44] He answers his own question:

"It is but to be brought from the material to the spiritual; . . . man must return to his forgotten inherent spirituality"[45] (emphasis his).

Referring to the Sublime Degree of Master Mason, Claudy comments: "The degree delves into the deepest recesses of a man's nature. While it leads the initiate into the Sanctum Sanctorum [Holy of Holies] of the Temple, it probes into the Holy of Holies of his heart.

"As a whole the degree is symbolical of that old age by the wisdom of which 'we may enjoy the happy reflection consequent on a well-spent life, and die in the hope of a glorious immortality.'"[46]

Notes in the Holman Masonic Bible say of the Master Mason, "The conclusion we arrive at is, that youth, properly directed, leads us to honorable and virtuous maturity, and that the life of man, regulated by morality, faith, and justice, will be rewarded at its closing hour, by the prospect of eternal bliss."[47] This is clearly a salvation by works, or character development—not a salvation by faith in Christ alone, who has paid the penalty for our sins.

Because Masons do not recognize the sinfulness of humanity, they see no need for salvation in the biblical sense. Former Mason Jim Shaw says of the Masonic doctrine of redemption: "Faith in the atonement of Jesus has nothing to do with it; it is rather a matter of enlightenment, step by step, which comes with initiation into the Masonic degrees and their mysteries."[48]

One of Shaw's great disillusionments with Masonry, however, was that when he got to the top as a serious seeker, he still did not find the Light he was looking for. When he took the 32nd Degree, he was told, "You have reached the mountain peak of Masonic instruction, a peak covered by a mist, which YOU in search for further light can penetrate only by your own efforts"[49] (emphasis his).

Biblical Christianity teaches that redemption is available only through the saving grace of the Lord Jesus Christ. "Nor is there salvation in any other, for there is no other name under heaven given among men by which we must be saved" (Acts 4:12).

Although any salvation of the Masons is sought through self-reformation, the Bible says, "By grace you have been saved through faith, and that not of yourselves; it is the gift of God, not of works, lest anyone should boast" (Eph. 2:8-9).

D. W. Kerr summarizes the Bible's teaching about the future life: "Immortality in the biblical sense is a condition in which the individual is not subject to death or to any influence which might lead to death."[50] He adds, "Immortality, for the Christian, involves the resurrection and may be fully attained only after it."[51]

The Masons speak of their three great beliefs: the Fatherhood of God, the brotherhood of man and the immortality of the soul. But what do they mean by the "immortality of the soul"? Masonry has little to say directly about immortality except through veiled references to it in other comments. And because Masons see immortality as a reward for character development, it is always uncertain whether they will receive the reward of immortality; or, if all are to receive the reward, what kind of a reward is it?

Conclusion

Serious conflict exists between biblical Christianity and Freemasonry. From the testimony of many of the leaders in Freemasonry about the spiritual views of Masons, there seems to be no way a man can be both a knowledgeable and committed Mason and a knowledgeable and committed Christian.

It is not surprising that churches with liberal theology see no conflict between Christianity and Freemasonry. If a church does not believe that the Bible is God's written revelation or that Jesus is God (a triune member of the one Godhead), or that salvation is available only through Him, it will see little apparent conflict with Masonry.

But it was a surpise to many evangelicals in June 1993 when delegates at the Southern Baptist Convention, after reading a seven-page report from its Home Mission Board, passed a resolution that "membership in a Masonic order [should] be a matter of personal conscience."[52]

If you are a Mason who endeavors to take your Christianity seriously, you've probably been surprised at the things you've read in this chapter. Perhaps you're thinking, *That's not what Masons believe.*

Don't take my word for it. Check the endnotes for references, and examine the Masonic sources for yourself. If you genuinely have the desire to find the true Light, you will be led to it. Ask the superiors at your lodge about the use of the Koran, the Vedas—and other holy books—as the Volume of the Sacred Law in non-Christian countries. Ask if the lodge is serious about following the specific teachings of the Bible or if it is only using it as a symbol. Ask your lodge leaders if they believe Jesus Christ is the only way of salvation.

What should a Bible-believing church do about admitting Masons to its membership and to leadership positions? Such a church should want only members and leaders who are believers and who are committed to following the Lord Jesus Christ.

In interviews for church membership and leadership, it is usually better to let the interviewee say what he believes rather than simply answering yes or no to a carefully worded doctrinal statement. For instance, rather than asking, "Do you believe that Jesus Christ is God and that salvation is available only through Him because of what He accomplished on the cross?" it is better to say, "Tell us what you believe about who Jesus Christ is and how a person can have forgiveness of sins and eternal life." Do not expect polished statements, of course, from a person without much theological background. But a Christian should be able to express the basics of what he believes.

Since Freemasonry sees itself as superseding and unifying all religions, a Mason may believe what he wants as long as he does not try to impose his views on others. This means that those who believe what a Bible-believing church teaches would be accepted as Masons as long as they do not insist their views are the only right ones.

Although it is better to let the interviewee respond in his or her own words, here are some suggested questions designed for yes-or-no answers that you might ask those who see no conflict between Freemasonry and Christianity:

1. Do you think that the Bible is God's written revelation to mankind and that it is the only such revelation?

2. Do you believe that Jesus Christ is God?

3. Do you believe that only the Bible explains how we can be saved from eternal condemnation?

4. Do you believe that trusting in Jesus Christ as Savior is the only way to obtain salvation?

5. Do you believe that Jesus Christ is the Light of the world and that all who do not follow Him walk in darkness, as John 8:12 says?

A knowledgeable and committed Mason would have to answer no to all of these questions if he is truthful. Freemasonry claims that nothing in it would offend the Christian, the Jew, the Muslim or the Brahmin—which means it cannot believe biblical truths about Jesus Christ. And because Freemasonry believes that only Masons are in the light and that all non-Masons are in darkness, no good Mason could say yes to the last question.

Be sure when dealing with a Mason—as with others—that you ask him to define his terms. What does he mean by such words as *God, Christ, light,* the *Fatherhood of God* and *salvation?* Freemasonry's mystical and metaphysical expressions are not easily understood, even by its own followers.

Perhaps the most significant issue for the person joining your church is that of authority. Matthew 6:24 says, "No one can serve two masters; for either he will hate the one and love the other; or else he will be loyal to the one and despise the other. You cannot serve God and mammon."

A Bible-teaching church needs to determine if an individual is giving total allegiance to Jesus Christ or to something else. A Mason has sworn allegiance to the religion of Freemasonry. Claiming that Christ is his Lord clearly presents a conflict with his Masonic beliefs.

While researching the beliefs of the Masons, I came into contact with an Air Force officer who had been a fourth-generation Mason. By the age of 23, he was a 32nd Degree Scottish Rite Prince of the Royal Secret, a York Rite Knight Templar, the Senior Deacon of a Blue Lodge that he attended and the unofficial Tyler of another lodge he frequently attended. He had been to lodges in New Hampshire, Arkansas, Oklahoma, Maine, Nebraska—even Japan and the Philippines. He not only attended but was active in most of these lodges. Of his own free will and accord he came to see that Jesus Christ was the true Light and the chief cornerstone that the builders had rejected (1 Pet. 2:6-7).

When he became a Master Mason, he was given a Masonic edition of the Bible. When he opened it, his eyes fell on Matthew 6:24, where he read that it is impossible to serve two masters. This caused him to think seriously about the conflicts that he knew existed between Freemasonry and Christianity. He eventually realized he had to forsake Masonry—which he had given allegiance to as his master—and follow only the Lord Jesus Christ. A well-read student of both Freemasonry and Christianity, he believes there is no possibility that a knowledgeable and committed Christian can also be a Mason.

Those faced with trying to assess to what extent Freemasonry conflicts with biblical Christianity should acquire books written by former Masons, such as those by Jim Shaw and Dale Byers (see Recommended Reading). These books, by those who have been there, reveal the darkness of Masonry.

Those who think the Bible and its teachings are taken seriously by Freemasonry need to be reminded of the words of Masonic authority Henry Wilson Coil: "The prevailing Masonic opinion is that the Bible is only a symbol of Divine Will, Law, or Revelation, and not that its contents are Divine Law, inspired, or revealed. So far, no responsible authority has held that a Freemason must believe the Bible or any part of it."[53]

SUMMARY

Name of organization:
Freemasonry

Also known as: Masons, Masonic Lodge

U.S. Headquarters: Alexandria, Virginia

U.S. Membership (1993): About 3.5 million

TWIST OR TRUTH?

SOURCE OF AUTHORITY

Freemasonry:

Uses the Bible *only* in a "Christian" lodge; the Hebrew Pentateuch in a Hebrew lodge; the Koran in a Muslim lodge; the Vedas in a Brahmin lodge. Pike said the Masonic search after light leads directly back to the Kabala.

Biblical Christianity:

Claims the Bible as the sole authority for beliefs and practices. Believes Jesus Christ is the only true Light.

GOD

Freemasonry:

Masonic candidate is never required to

say what God he believes in, for "Freemasonry cares not." Explains deity as Grand Artificer, Grand Master of the Grand Lodge Above, Jehovah, Allah, Buddha, Brahma, Vishnu, Shiva or Great Geometer.

Biblical Christianity:

Defines God in terms and descriptions found in the Bible. Believes that God shares His glory with none other.

JESUS CHRIST

Freemasonry:

Omits references to Jesus Christ when quoting from the Bible. Does not care whether a person privately petitions God or Jehovah, Allah or Buddha, Mohammed or Jesus, the God of Israel or the Great First Cause; but in the lodge they petition only the Great Architect of the Universe.

Biblical Christianity:

Believes that the death, burial and resurrection of Jesus Christ is the special focus of Christianity. Believes that all access to God is through the Lord Jesus Christ because of His finished work on the cross.

SIN

Freemasonry:

Denies the reality of sin in the biblical sense; believes any shortcomings can be overcome by greater enlightenment.

Biblical Christianity:

Believes sin to be any act or character that fails to measure up to God's standard, and that all have sinned and come short of God's glory.

SALVATION

Freemasonry:

Teaches a salvation by works or character development.

Biblical Christianity:

Believes salvation is by grace through faith in the finished work of the Lord Jesus Christ, apart from works.

RECOMMENDED READING

Ankerberg, John, and Weldon, John. *The Facts on the Masonic Lodge.* Eugene, Ore.: Harvest House, 1988.

__________. *The Secret Teachings of the Masonic Lodge.* Chicago: Moody Press, 1990.

Byers, Dale. *I Left the Lodge.* Schaumburg, Ill.: Regular Baptist Press, 1988.

Mather, George A., and Nichols, Larry A. *Masonic Lodge.* Grand Rapids, Mich.: Zondervan Publishing House, 1995.

McClain, Alva J. *Freemasonry and Christianity.* Winona Lake, Ind.: BMH Books, 1979.

Rongstad, L. James. *The Lodge*, rev. ed. St. Louis: Concordia Publishing House, 1995.

Shaw, Jim, and McKenney, Tom. *The Deadly Deception: Freemasonry Exposed . . . by One of Its Top Leaders.* Lafayette, La.: Huntington House, Inc., 1988.

NOTES

[1] *Christianity Today*, May 17, 1993, p. 81.

[2] Associated Baptist Press, cited in *Christianity Today*, May 17, 1993, p. 81.

[3] L. James Rongstad, *How to Respond to . . . the Lodge* (St. Louis: Concordia Publishing House, 1977), p. 10.

[4] William J. Whalen, *Handbook of Secret Organizations* (Milwaukee: The Bruce Publishing Company, 1966), pp. 43-44.

[5] Dale A. Byers, *I Left the Lodge: A Former Mason Tells Why* (Schaumburg, Ill.: Regular Baptist Press, 1988), pp. 17-18.

[6] Henry C. Clausen, 33rd Degree, *To a Non-Mason: You Must Seek Masonic Membership!* (Washington, D.C.: The Supreme Council, 33rd Degree, Mother Council of the World, Ancient and Accepted Scottish Rite of Freemasonry, Southern Jurisdiction, U.S.A., report, 1984), p. 4.

[7] Henry Wilson Coil, 33rd Degree, *Coil's Masonic Encyclopedia* (New York: Macoy Publishing & Masonic Supply Company, Inc., 1961), p. 266.

[8] Ibid., p. 631.

[9] Carl H. Claudy, *Introduction to Freemasonry*, Vol. II (Washington, D.C.: The Temple Publishers, 1943), pp. 55-56.

[10] Elliott Miller, "Saying No to the New Age," *Moody Monthly*, February 1985, p. 25.

[11] Joseph Fort Newton, *The Religion of Masonry: An Interpretation* (Richmond, Va.: Macoy Publishing & Masonic Supply Company, Inc., 1969), p. 11.

[12] Ibid., p. 12.

[13] Ibid., p. 34

[14] Ankerberg and Weldon, *The Facts on the Masonic Lodge: Does Masonry Conflict with the Christian Faith?* (Eugene, Ore.: Harvest House Publishers, Inc., 1989), pp. 8-9.

[15] Coil, *Coil's Masonic Encyclopedia*, p. 512.

[16] Ibid.

[17] Ibid.

[18] Albert Pike, *Morals and Dogma of the Ancient and Accepted Scottish Rite of Freemasonry* (Charleston, S.C.: Supreme Council of the Thirty-Third Degree, 1905), p. 11.

[19] Claudy, *Introduction to Freemasonry,* Vol. I, p. 37.

[20] Ibid.

[21] Jim Shaw and Tom McKenney, *The Deadly Deception: Freemasonry Exposed . . . by One of Its Top Leaders* (Lafayette, La.: Huntington House, Inc., 1988), p. 128.

[22] Coil, *Coil's Masonic Encyclopedia*, p. 111.

[23] Ibid.

[24] Joseph Fort Newton, *The Builders: A Story and Study of Freemasonry* (Richmond, Va.: Macoy Publishing & Masonic Supply Company, Inc., 1979), p. 146.

[25] Ibid., p. 147.

[26] Pike, *Morals and Dogma*, p. 15.

[27] Ibid., p. 17.

[28] Ibid., p. 741.

[29] George A. Mather and Larry A. Nichols, *Masonic Lodge* (Grand Rapids, Mich.: Zondervan Publishing House, 1995), p. 24.

[30] Claudy, *Introduction to Freemasonry*, Vol. II, pp. 109-110.

[31] Ibid., p. 110.

[32] Ibid.

[33] Ibid.

[34] Ibid., p. 109.

[35] Holy Bible: Masonic Edition (Philadelphia: A. J. Holman Company, 1951), p. 21.

[36] Ibid., p. 20.

[37] George H. Steinmetz, *The Lost Word: Its Hidden Meaning* (Richmond, Va.: Macoy Publishing & Masonic Supply Company, 1953), pp. 135-136.

[38] Ibid, p. 136.

[39] Ibid., p. 155.

[40] Ibid.

[41] Shaw and McKenney, *The Deadly Deception*, p. 152.

[42] Claudy, *Introduction to Freemasonry*,

Vol. I, p. 38.

[43] Holy Bible: Masonic Edition, p. 22.

[44] Steinmetz, *The Lost Word*, p. 156.

[45] Ibid., p. 157.

[46] Claudy, *Introduction to Freemasonry*, Vol. III, p. 125.

[47] Holy Bible: Masonic Edition, p. 22.

[48] Shaw and McKenney, *The Deadly Deception*, p. 132.

[49] Ibid., p. 157.

[50] D. W. Kerr, "Immortality" in *Evangelical Dictionary of Theology*, Walter A. Elwell, ed. (Grand Rapids, Mich.: Baker Book House, 1984), pp. 551-552.

[51] Ibid., p. 552.

[52] Timothy C. Morgan in *Christianity Today*, July 19, 1993, p. 54.

[53] Coil, *Coil's Masonic Encyclopedia*, p. 520.